MASS APPEAL

MASS APPEAL

BILL C. DAVIS

AVON
PUBLISHERS OF BARD, CAMELOT AND DISCUS BOOKS

MASS APPEAL was chosen for circulation by Plays in Process, a project of Theater Communications Group, Inc., the national service organization for the nonprofit professional theatre.

AVON BOOKS
A division of
The Hearst Corporation
959 Eighth Avenue
New York, New York 10019

Copyright © 1981 by Bill C. Davis
Published by arrangement with the author

Photographs by Gerry Goodstein

Printed in the U.S.A.

MASS APPEAL

by
Bill C. Davis

received its World Premiere
at the Manhattan Theatre Club
April 22, 1980

with

(in alphabetical order)
MILO O'SHEA   ERIC ROBERTS

Directed by
Geraldine Fitzgerald

Set Design
David Gropman

Costume Design
William Ivey Long

Lighting Design
F. Mitchell Dana

THE SETTING

The action of the play takes place in Father
Tim Farley's office and in St. Francis Church.
It is autumn.

CHARACTERS

FATHER TIM FARLEY
MARK DOLSON

ACT ONE

The church. TIM *is in the pulpit. It is Sunday morning.*

TIM: Today we are concluding our 3-C series. For new-comers here at St. Francis, that's "Current Crises in Catholicism." Our next series will be the most important and inspiring I've ever given. I don't know what it is yet but it will begin next Sunday—so don't miss it. Last night, while I was thinking about our 3-C series, I fell asleep straining over the most recent issue facing our church today. Consequently, I dreamt that Bette Davis was ordained a priest. You guessed it—the question we have to ask ourselves this morning is: Should women be priests? I remember when the *big* moral question of the day was, "Should we chew the host or let it melt in our mouths?" I think that today's crisis is controversial enough that we could open this up to a—dialogue sermon. Now I'm sure you've all done some thinking about this and we've had dialogue sermons before. They can be lots of fun if we're not shy, so let's . . . [*Points to left*] Yes—Mrs. Curry. [*He listens*] Well—the reason the pope gives is that priests should be in the image of Christ. Now this is what *he* says

1

and he is not speaking ex cathedra. In other words, that decision is not infallible. So there's still hope for you, Mrs. Curry. [*Points*] Yes—Mrs. Hart. [*He listens*] No—that does not mean I'll have to grow a beard, Mrs. Hart. And even if I had to, I wouldn't. A beard would make me look at least ten years older. [*Points*] Yes—in the back.
[MARK DOLSON *steps forward*]

MARK: What do *you* think of women becoming priests?

TIM: What do *I* think? Well . . . I don't like to sway people's viewpoints so I'll plead the fifth on that one.

MARK: Yes—but this is a dialogue sermon.

TIM: I know it's a dialogue sermon.

MARK: And dialogue means . . .

TIM: I know what dialogue means. Is this your first visit to our church?

MARK: Yes.

TIM: Well—welcome. [*Points*] Yes—Mr. Quinn.

MARK: I haven't given my unswayed viewpoint yet.

TIM: That's true—you haven't.

MARK: I think women should be priests.

TIM: You look awfully familiar. Where are you from?

MARK: I attend St. Francis Seminary.

TIM: That's where I've seen you before. Give my regards to your rector, Monsignor Burke when you see him. Now— Mr. Quinn.

MARK: Don't you want to know *why* I think women should be priests?

TIM: [*Pause*] By all means—don't be shy.

MARK: Well—you said that priests should be in the image of Christ.

TIM: I didn't say that. The pope did.

MARK: Whoever. But when Christ was crucified, only three people stayed with him to the very end and two of the three were women. At the foot of the cross was his youngest apostle . . . his mother, and an ex-hooker. All of the men either denied him or were hiding out. On the way to being crucified—it was a woman who pushed through a very hostile crowd and wiped all the blood and "male" spit off his face. The first person he appeared to after his resurrection was Mary Magdalene. I really feel that the courage and loyalty these women showed to the actual person Jesus *is* in his image, and I think it's foolish to continue depriving ourselves of the beautiful qualities a woman could bring to the priesthood.

TIM: You really should invest in a portable pulpit. Now— Mr. Quinn. [*Silence*] You forgot what you were going to say? Well— [*Looks to* MARK] That happens. Anyone else? [*Silence*] No one? [*Pause*] Oh come on—I saw some hands up before . . . [*Silence*] Aaaaaalright. I have two announcements this morning. There's bingo this Tuesday

3

night in Mother Cabrini Hall—or Cabrini's Casino as I prefer to call it. And whoever has a blue Seville, license number DU–947—please move it—you're blocking the exit. I'd strongly advise whoever you are to move the car as soon as possible, because after mass a church exit is the most dangerous passage in the world. Let us pray.
[*Lights down on pulpit and up on the office where* MARK *is waiting in a sweat suit and sneakers.* TIM *enters*]

TIM: So—Mark Dolson—

MARK: Father Farley—

TIM: I only have a few minutes, but this won't take long. [*Noticing* MARK'*s sweat suit*] Is this the new uniform for seminarians?

MARK: I wasn't sure I should come in dressed this way, but . . .

TIM: [*Looking at his sneakers*] I hope you didn't track mud through Margaret's nice clean floors.

MARK: Sorry.

TIM: Was it necessary that you run here?

MARK: I try to keep a schedule—eight miles a day. It's four miles between here and the seminary, and I'll run the other four when I leave.

TIM: I'm glad you could fit me in.

MARK: It's just that I always do the eight miles around this

4

time. When you called, I said "yes" to this time without thinking.

TIM: There's actually a time when you're not thinking?

MARK: Sometimes, I think more clearly than at other times. When I'm on the phone I don't think very clearly.

TIM: You think very clearly at mass.

MARK: I feel at home in church.

TIM: Yes—that was very apparent on Sunday. [*Pause*] Tell me—why do you think women are better than men?

MARK: I didn't say they were better. They're more loyal.

TIM: What makes you say that?

MARK: Is this why you wanted to see me?

TIM: Do you know I am an advisor at your seminary?

MARK: Yes—Father DeNicola plays tapes of your sermons in our homily class and the faculty talk about you a lot. They seem proud that you're on their "team." But I never see you there.

TIM: The parish keeps me busy. Anyway—I asked some of the faculty about you and from my description of you they knew you instantly. And from what they say, you have quite a reputation.

MARK: Really?

TIM: And you lived up to that reputation Sunday.

MARK: Did I?

TIM: Yes—and so I wanted to tell you how much I admired the things you were saying during my mass, and don't ever do anything like that again.

MARK: Why not?

TIM: You were challenging me in front of my congregation. I don't like that.

MARK: I took a stand.

TIM: No you didn't. You took a *grand*stand. Besides—you're a seminarian—and if you want to become a deacon, you should be going to mass at the seminary.

MARK: Believe me—I prefer going to mass at the seminary.

TIM: Then why didn't you?

MARK: Because the rector sent me to yours.

TIM: Monsignor Burke?

MARK: Yes.

TIM: Monsignor Burke sent you to my mass?

MARK: Yes.

TIM: Did he say why he was sending you?

MARK: He said that you were the most tactful priest in the diocese, and that tact was something I needed to learn.

TIM: [*Laughs*] He is really something.

MARK: You're not the most tactful priest in the diocese?

TIM: I might be—but that's not why he sent you.

MARK: It's not?

TIM: No.

MARK: Well—why do *you* think he sent me?

TIM: Because he wanted to get back at me for cancelling a dinner engagement with him.

MARK: I'm sorry—I don't understand.

TIM: He gets very upset when I cancel anything with him, but he'll never show it. So he does something more subtle. He knows your reputation—he knows my dialogue sermons, so he put them together hoping for exactly what happened. In other words, you did what he wanted you to do.

MARK: If I was used as a pawn, that's the players' problem, not mine.

TIM: If you want to be a priest in the same church as the players, it is your problem.

MARK: Do you cancel dinners with him often?

TIM: Is that any of your business?

MARK: You just said—it is my problem. I should get to know

7

the church hierarchy—monsignors, advisors—why did you cancel?

TIM: Someone from the parish was having a problem. I couldn't get away.

MARK: Really?

TIM: You don't believe that.

MARK: No.

TIM: Very good. You shouldn't. Actually—he and his sister had pictures from a trip the three of us took to Yugoslavia. And they wanted to get together with me over dinner to look at the pictures.

MARK: Why didn't you?

TIM: The only thing I can imagine worse than the trip itself would be pictures of the trip. [*Silence*] It was a harmless lie.

MARK: I didn't know there was such a thing.

TIM: Well—worse than that—it was a useless lie. [TIM *laughs*]

MARK: Can I go now? It's not good to break up the eight miles this much.

TIM: If you'd rather skip the rest of your run, I could give you a lift. I have to go to the seminary anyway. I have a meeting with Monsignor Burke. About two seminarians. Maybe you might know something. Frank Kearney and Alfred Virasi—do you know them?

MARK: Yeah—fairly well. They work with the emotionally disturbed children every Tuesday and Thursday. I watch them—they're good.

TIM: They're together a lot.

MARK: They're best friends.

TIM: How do you know?

MARK: I usually see them with each other during the day, so I assume . . .

TIM: I probably shouldn't be discussing this with you, but this meeting was prompted by rumors reaching Monsignor Burke that not only are they together all day, but all night as well. Do you know if that's so?

MARK: No—I don't. But so what if they are?

TIM: Don't play innocent Mark. When I was in the seminary we could only travel in threes. Things have loosened up a little, but there are still strong tabus. Frank and Alfred are fooling around with the ultimate tabu.

MARK: They haven't taken any vows yet.

TIM: There's serious question they'll be allowed to—ever.

MARK: That's ridiculous—one meeting can't decide that.

TIM: You're right—meetings don't decide anything. They only help Monsignor Burke decide.

MARK: How are you going to advise him?

9

TIM: The only purpose of the rector's advisor is to find out what the rector really wants to do and then advise him to do that.

MARK: That must make you feel awfully insignificant.

TIM: I'd love to discuss this with you further, but if I don't leave now, I'll be late. And the one thing he loves more than chastity is punctuality. Are you sure you don't want a lift?

MARK: Is that your Mercedes out front?

TIM: Yes.

MARK: I'd rather run. [*He starts to leave but stops*] Listen— I don't know if your and Monsignor Burke's game-rules apply to seminarians, but I hope you won't use your position at the seminary over me. I only spoke up at your mass because it was important to me. Becoming a priest is important to me. Please don't play games with it. [MARK *exits.* TIM *is still*]

[BLACKOUT. *In the dark we hear a recording of* FARLEY's *voice*]

TIM: This Thursday—the rector and I and the faculty of St. Francis Seminary will have our final meeting to decide which of the seminarians will become deacons. So what better time to begin our "On the Road to the Priesthood Series" . . .
[*Lights up on* TIM *in his office preparing a sermon with the use of a tape recorder*]

Mass Appeal

. . . A deacon must take a vow of celibacy. He can then preach, give out communion, visit the sick, teach religion and counsel. Being a deacon is primarily and most importantly a big pain in the . . . neck. There is a rumor going around the parish that I was *born* a priest. This is not true. I too passed through the many phases required by the priesthood. The most horrible for me was being a deacon. One day a week, for an entire summer, as part of my training, I had to give sermons from a soap box on a street corner. Can you picture that? From where I was standing, it looked as if the only people who stopped to listen were members of the House Un-American Activities Committee. Every Sunday was hot and humid. I wanted to wear sunglasses because instinctively I knew squinting would not help my charisma. But sunglasses weren't allowed. So I wore a hat. And all the members of the House Un-American Activities Committee wore hats. And there we were—once a week—all peering out at each other. But other people did stop. Shoppers, students, workers on their lunch hours—all kinds of people. And we . . . talked. Isn't it funny? I don't remember so much what they said—as much as I remember what they wore. They were just regular, everyday people. Women in light-colored dresses—young men in shorts—old men in faded plaid shirts—just about everyone wore some kind of sandal, and I know I haven't been as close to Christ—since.

[*Lights out in office. The tape recorder repeats* TIM's *voice*]

TIM's voice: —old men in faded plaid shirts—just about everyone wore some kind of sandal, and I know I haven't been as close to Christ—since.

[*House phone buzzes.*

Lights up on the office. TIM *answers*]

11

TIM: Yes Margaret . . . Good. Send him in. [*He hangs up. MARK enters and stands at doorway. He is again dressed in his sweat suit*]

TIM: I see you're still in uniform.

MARK: Hello Father.

TIM: Come in.

MARK: [*Staying at the doorway*] Did you want to see me about something important?

TIM: Tell me—do you do any exercising besides the running?

MARK: Yes.

TIM: Working out your hostilities?

MARK: No—I don't have any hostilities; I'm preparing for celibacy.

TIM: You may not have to.

MARK: What did you say?

TIM: You may not have to prepare for celibacy—or the priesthood.

MARK: What are you talking about?

TIM: Monsignor Burke has been having second thoughts about several seminarians. During our final meeting—your name came up.

MARK: Why?

TIM: He said that you were immature, and he felt very strongly that you weren't ready to be a deacon.

MARK: He has no reason to say that.

TIM: He suggested you take a year off to think about whether or not you really want to be a priest, which, as you'll learn, is Latin for "get lost."

MARK: I'll kill him.

TIM: But without hostility, of course.

MARK: [*Going to leave*] I'm going to talk to him.

TIM: Mark—wait.

MARK: Am I being used as a pawn again?

TIM: No.

MARK: Then why are you telling me all this? Why isn't Monsignor Burke?

TIM: I'll explain, if you'll slow down.

MARK: I thought everything was decided.

TIM: It was.

MARK: What happened?

TIM: Don't you know?

MARK: No—I don't.

TIM: I spoke to Monsignor Burke after the meeting, which is when all the real issues come out, and he said that this past Wednesday, you stormed into his office and attacked him on his decision to force a leave of absence on Frank Kearney and Alfred Virasi.

MARK: I didn't attack. I expressed my opinion.

TIM: And in the course of expressing your opinion, did you call him a "homophobic autocrat"?

MARK: Yes.

TIM: If you want to become a priest, you can't do things like that.

MARK: I had to.

TIM: Why do you feel you must be the knight-errant?

MARK: You're never at the seminary. You don't see it. Nobody there cares what's going on. Do you know how many seminarians have TVs in their rooms? Most of their praying and meditating is done during commercials. They all drive brand-new freshly simonized cars. They take off to St. Thomas and California like I go to the movies. But that's fine with Monsignor Burke. Somehow that fits in with his definition of ecumenism. But he hears a few rumors about Frank and Alfred and he gets out his trumpet to blow down the walls of Sodom and Gomorrah.

TIM: Mark—save it. I spoke to Monsignor Burke on your behalf, and you're going to be made a deacon this Wednesday, just like the rest of them. But from what I can see so far—you aren't like the rest of them.

MARK: I'm not so different.

TIM: You've just been implying that you are.

MARK: [*Pause*] Thank you for your help with Monsignor Burke.

TIM: It's all right. [*Silence*]

MARK: Is there anything else?

TIM: As a matter of fact—there is. My good deed did not go unpunished. You've been assigned to me.

MARK: What?

TIM: You've been assigned to me. Monsignor Burke let you by with reservation and on condition that I work with you.

MARK: I don't want to be a special assignment.

TIM: Fine—then you won't become a deacon, and I'll have less work.

MARK: [*Pause*] What does he think you'll teach me that I won't be taught at the seminary?

TIM: Contrary to what you may think, I am considered to be one of the best priests in this diocese. I'm not bragging —that's just how things are.

15

MARK: You're popular—that doesn't mean you can teach me what I need to learn.

TIM: Oh—you don't want to be popular?

MARK: No.

TIM: Do you want to be a priest?

MARK: Yes.

TIM: Then shut up and do what I tell you. [*Pause*] Before we begin—as a rule—is this day good for you? Friday?

MARK: No.

TIM: All right—what about Thursday?

MARK: No good either.

TIM: Why not?

MARK: The senior citizen center has a dance every Thursday afternoon and I play the piano for them.

TIM: I see. Wednesday?

MARK: No.

TIM: What happens on Wednesday?

MARK: Meals on wheels.

TIM: What on earth is "meals on wheels"?

MARK: It's a program for shut-ins. People in the community bring dinners to people who can't get out.

TIM: How about Tuesday?

MARK: Prison.

TIM: So Tuesday's no good either. Well Monday is no good for me. I go to the races. I go to the races on Monday to get over the masses on Sunday. So that leaves today. Now tell me I'm keeping you from a leper colony. [MARK *is silent*] Let's just decide every Friday so we can get to work. [*Dials intercom*] Margaret—I have one appointment this afternoon I will have to cancel . . . Never mind why. Mr. and Mrs. Koyn—they're worried because they haven't had a fight in twenty-three years. Margaret—listen. I made the appointment with Mrs. Koyn so tell Mr. Koyn that she mixed up the date. See if that gets anything started . . . It's not a lie, Margaret. It's creative counseling . . . Now Margaret—we've talked about your scruples before . . . All right, all right. Just tell the Koyns to call me next week. Thank you, Margaret. [*He hangs up*] The word scruples comes from the Latin meaning pebbles, Margaret is a veritable boulder. Now I've talked with the faculty and I've met with Monsignor Burke—over dinner you'll be happy to hear. And from these meetings I've broken down our work into three lessons.

MARK: "Lessons"—what is this? Remedial reading?

TIM: It's structure.

MARK: I'm all for structure—but "lessons"?

TIM: You can call them what you like—I'm calling them lessons. Lesson I—Sermons. At some point, you'll be expected to give a sermon. Father DeNicola gave me some of your sermons from his class, which I haven't had a chance to read. Let's take your most recent one and go over that together.

[TIM *pulls it out of folder and hands it to* MARK. TIM *then takes the* prie-dieu *and sets it up as a "rehearsal pulpit"*] Now step into the rehearsal pulpit and let's hear it.

MARK: The rehearsal pulpit?

TIM: [*Patting it*] The rehearsal pulpit. You do have it memorized?

MARK: Yes—but you have it right there. Can't you just read it?

TIM: I have to hear your technique.

MARK: My technique?

TIM: Yes—I've seen what you can do when someone else is in the pulpit, but it's different when you're in there yourself.

MARK: [*Positions himself behind the rehearsal pulpit*] Jesus is not impressed with your mink hats and your cashmere coats and your blue hair . . .

TIM: Never say "you" and "your." It's "we" and "our"—always. [*Pencils in changes*]

MARK: What are you doing?

18

TIM: Making the correction. Go on.

MARK: Jesus is not impressed with *our* mink hats and *our* cashmere coats and . . . our blue hair?

TIM: Cut the "blue hair." Go on.

MARK: Those things are our shackles. They dim our vision. They . . . they . . . What's the rest?

TIM: Skip it. If you can't remember a part of a sentence, it usually doesn't belong. Go on.

MARK: How far can we go? How long before light and air can't penetrate the clutter of objects with which you . . . with which we shower ourselves.

TIM: Scratch the "with which." Just say "which we shower ourselves with."

MARK: Sermons can't be grammatically correct?

TIM: They should be understood. Proper grammar doesn't necessarily help understanding.

MARK: And I don't shower myself with objects.

TIM: Your family does.

MARK: How do you know that?

TIM: Monsignor Burke showed me your family's official Christmas card: a massive fireplace, Chippendale furniture, and a smiling English setter picturesquely posed by the roaring hearth.

MARK: Maybe my family showers themselves with objects, but I don't. And I don't wear mink hats. Why do I have to say "we"?

TIM: I'm only telling you what works.

MARK: And if "what works" isn't the truth? . . .

TIM: Mark—do you like my sermons?

MARK: Well . . . No.

TIM: What do you mean, "well . . . no"? I have to sign autographs after every mass.

MARK: I never liked song and dance theology.

TIM: I see. Monsignor Burke is a homophobic autocrat and I'm Father Bojangles.

MARK: Maybe things were different when you were growing up, but when I was a teenager, the church was a circus. Everyone sang Top 40 tunes at mass. Didn't matter if they related. I remember once, on Ascension Thursday— the day Jesus ultimately transcends the world, and body and soul enters heaven—the hip hymn committee sang "Leavin' on a Jet Plane." In grammar school, the religion teacher's bible was the "Gospel according to Peanuts." So I grew up thinking Jesus was a beagle. Let me say what I want from the pulpit. I think people respect that. They feel more secure with someone who states his position clearly.

TIM: State it as clearly as you like. If it's not their position, they'll turn on you.

MARK: Then the only reason you give sermons is to be liked?

TIM: I like being liked. It gives me a warm feeling. That and wine are the only warmth I get. I'm not about to give up either.

MARK: You'll be liked much more for being real and sober.

TIM: Well—this is a great way to begin. So far, you have called me a song and dance theologian, a phony and a drunkard. I am your teacher.

MARK: I respect standards—not positions.

TIM: Fine—you don't have to respect my position or me. But the one thing I insist you respect is my congregation. You'll be giving a sermon during my mass, and I'll tell you straight off—you're not giving this "kick-ass" sermon to my congregation.

MARK: A congregation that keeps you well stocked in sparkling Burgundy. And why do you drink so much?

TIM: I have never missed a mass, a class or an appointment in my entire career as a priest. Never.

MARK: You just cancelled one . . .

TIM: Cancelling is not missing. And I'll have you know further, that in this past week alone, this drunken minstrel met and dealt with four broken marriages, ten identity crises, three potential abortions and seven "I don't know why I'm alive's."

MARK: And I bet you were too easy on all of them. If you give them a hard time they might get annoyed. So I'm sure you say just what they want to hear. It's what you do from the pulpit.

TIM: The pulpit is not the place to ventilate.

MARK: I know—but there are serious moral and social conditions that can be tended to from the pulpit.

TIM: Mark—your sermon sucks.

MARK: You haven't heard the rest.

TIM: The rest could be the Sermon on the Mount, but after two minutes of this they would have turned you off.

MARK: I can't believe that.

TIM: It's not a question of faith. It's the cold hard facts of the pulpit.

MARK: What are you suggesting I do?

TIM: I'm not suggesting—I'm telling you—don't kick ass.

MARK: Better that than to kiss it.
[TIM *tears up the sermon.*
MARK *goes to leave*]

TIM: Mark—I'm doing this for your own good. Monsignor Burke can keep you as a deacon for the next ten years. The only thing that can influence him more than I can is the congregation. So you have to give a friendly sermon. Every sermon needs a theme. There are "what if" sermons; there are "remember when" sermons; and there are "why" sermons. "Why" sermons are the most fundamental. So we'll start you off on a "why" sermon. Your theme will be "Why go to mass?"

MARK: "Why go to mass?"

TIM: Yes. And don't be afraid to be charming. There's nothing wrong with being charming. Be personal. Talk about yourself. For example—did your family go to mass together?

MARK: Yes—but . . .

TIM: Did you wear a suit?

MARK: What difference would that make?

TIM: They need to see you in a nice Norman Rockwell setting. Did you wear a suit?

MARK: Yes—well, not really a suit—it was more like an outfit.

TIM: An outfit.

MARK: Yeah—you know.

TIM: No—I don't.

MARK: Well—I had a red sportscoat—with gold buttons—they looked like Roman coins. And a vest—houndstooth check—and a clip-on tie because I couldn't tie a regular tie.

TIM: Were you good in church?

MARK: No.

TIM: Even then. What would you do that was so bad?

MARK: I'd laugh a lot.

TIM: Why?

MARK: Well—you know—something would strike me funny. Someone would make a noise—or a baby would throw his mother's hat in the aisle—and I'd laugh—and knowing I wasn't supposed to made it that much harder to stop—and trying to stop just sent me into hysterics. A few times my father had to pull me outside.

TIM: Did he hit you?

MARK: No—he never hit me.

TIM: That's good.

MARK: He shook me a few times. Why did you ask that? Is that part of your Norman Rockwell setting?

TIM: No. None of this really is. What about after mass? Where would you and your family go after mass?

MARK: The bakery.

TIM: Really? Now that's more like it. That's nice. What would you get?

MARK: Jelly doughnuts.

TIM: Great! Now that's the kind of thing you have to go for.

MARK: People don't come to mass to hear about bakeries.

TIM: Mark—I've been at this for a while and that's exactly what they want to hear. And they're going to hear it the first Sunday there's an opening in our calendar of Sunday events. So I want you to be ready immediately.

MARK: Immediately?

TIM: Yes—cancellations can come at any minute. So back to the seminary and get to work on your jelly-doughnut sermon.
[MARK *turns to leave in a daze*]
Oh—one more thing—very important—you must always have an alternate sermon ready in case the one you're giving isn't working.

MARK: How will I know if it's not working?

TIM: Coughs.

MARK: Coughs?

TIM: Yes. If you hear a lot of coughs it means they're bored, so watch out for that. And if they start dropping their missals, you're in trouble too. Missal-dropping is a subconscious way of turning you off. It's a *dis*missal of you.

MARK: That is the most ridiculous thing I've heard you say. How can the spirit move me if I'm listening for coughs and people dropping books?

TIM: The "spirit" moving you. Mark—here are the facts of this particular campaign we're about to embark on. If the people in my parish think you're cute and witty, this will find its way to Monsignor Burke, who in turn will begin proceedings for your canonization. But if the people in my parish think you are what we used to call at the seminary a "Bangla Desh Granola Head," this too will find its way to Monsignor Burke and you'll be immediately shipped off to a rustic bakery in the mountains with the Trappists. Now, those are your choices.

MARK: What do they bake there?

[BLACKOUT. *The church.* TIM *is in the pulpit.*]

TIM: All right—let's get back to our seats. You've been shaking hands for fifteen minutes and the diocesan manual says anything past ten can be considered indecent. Today —we were supposed to see Sister Rosalie and her Maryknoll Marionettes. But Sister Claire accidentally slammed the car door on Sister Rosalie's hand. Nothing serious— ~~BUT~~ but she operates the bottom part of the puppet with that hand, so we'll have to wait. [*He stops*] As I look around this morning I see we have some of the faculty from St. Francis Seminary here. And I have a treat for all of you. In keeping with our "On the Road to the Priesthood Series," we're going to hear a first sermon. This is a young man who was just installed as a deacon this past Wednesday. Some of you might remember him from our last dialogue sermon. There's a certain James Dean quality about him which I think you'll find very exciting. Will you welcome please—Deacon Dolson. [TIM *leaves the pulpit.* MARK *enters*]

MARK: Thank you Father Farley. It's funny—I never stopped to think that on my way to becoming a priest I'd have to live with the name, Deacon Dolson. It sounds pretty silly, don't you think? "Deacon Dolson." [*A cough*

26

—he freezes] Can I ask all of you a question? Why did you come to mass today? What brought you to church this morning? As a teenager I had a friend who answered this question by saying, "I go to mass because my parents go." But one day, I heard his father talking to my father: "Betty and I go to mass because of the kids." [*Coughs*] I know when I was young, I liked going to church because right after mass my father would take us to the bakery. And all four of us—my two sisters and my brother and myself—would pick out what we'd like. I'd almost always get jelly dougnuts, and I'd never wait to get home before having one . . . [*Coughs*] Anyway—jelly doughnuts aren't a very good reason for going to mass, are they? [*A missal drops*] What are your reasons . . . [*Coughs*] I wonder if the coughing lot of you know, or *try* to know why you pull yourselves out of bed every Sunday morning and come here!? [*Silence*] Do you need to come to mass? Do you need the church? Ideally, the purpose of the church is to become obsolete. But until it is, we need the habit of coming together and collectively recognizing that there is another world. There is a world that coexists and gives order to this world. Individually, we come to mass with our own personal chaos and together we look to be ordered. We must come with our hearts open for that. [*Cough*] But you come here with your mink hats and your cashmere coats and your blue hair—that doesn't change anything. Those things are your shackles—they are accessories you've made essential—you are essential. You come here a faceless mass—you wear your prison uniforms as if they were badges. You're slaves all week—do you want to be slaves here too . . .

[*Rapid* CROSS FADE.
The office. TIM *is on the phone.*]

TIM: Yes—well, he's very high-spirited—like a thoroughbred at the starting gate . . . I know you come to mass because of me, Helen, but he has to start somewhere. I mean, if he were going to be a dentist, there would have to be that first set of molars . . . I know you're not a molar, Helen. I, for one, have always thought of you as a bicuspid . . . [*He listens for her laugh; then he laughs. House phone buzzes*] Listen—I have to run, Helen. Oh—and thanks again for the "bubbly" and thank Jim for me, will you. Yes—don't worry—I'll be speaking to him very soon. You bet. Thanks for calling, Helen. [*Presses intercom button*] Yes Margaret . . . Good. Send him in.

[MARK *enters*]

Well, Mark—the parish poll is in and eighty percent of those interviewed, after having seen the spirit move you, feel that you and the spirit should move each other to the bakery in the mountains. But take heart. You might be able to convince the Trappists to expand the bakery—then you could have jelly doughnuts *every* day.

MARK: Why did you invite faculty?

TIM: I didn't invite them. They came to see Sister Rosalie and her Maryknoll Marionettes. And they were surprised and thrilled to hear that the purpose of the church is to become obsolete.

MARK: The faculty doesn't matter. You said that the people decide.

TIM: They do.

MARK: Well—they stopped coughing.

TIM: They also stopped breathing. [*Phone buzzes.* TIM *answers phone*] Yes Margaret . . . Tell him I'm out . . . Margaret . . . This is no time for scruples. I can't deal with Mr. Hartigan right now . . . All right, Margaret . . . All right—then let me get to him before he gets angry for being kept waiting. [*Presses button*] Hello Mr. Hartigan . . . Oh you were . . . Yes—he's a deacon. Yes—well he's very high-spirited—like a thoroughbred at the starting gate . . . I know the church is not a racetrack, Mr. Hartigan . . . I'm sorry he made you uncomfortable . . . I know you worked hard for everything you own, but I don't think he was denying that . . . I agree—there's no reason you should feel shackled . . . Yes—I got the bottle of sparkling Burgundy you and Mrs. Hartigan sent me. Thank you and thank her for me, will you? . . . No—not at all—I'm glad you called. It's always good to know the pulse of the parish. Good-bye, Mr. Hartigan. [*He hangs up and is visibly shaken*]

MARK: Why do you let them do that to you?

TIM: Mark—when I first came here, the people didn't want me. The priest I replaced was well loved and nobody was happy about his transfer. I was compared to him—the men ignored me—the women were painfully polite to me. Rich men in sick beds chastised me for not coming to visit sooner. I would come home to my room after my daily rounds and throw things. I would go to bed at 11:00 and maybe fall asleep by 4:00. I broke out in a rash everywhere on my body except my hands and face. And whatever it was that kept the rash off my hands and face got me through. And I have achieved a level of beloved— a level I have basked in for the past ten years and for which I have never had to fight as hard as I had to this morning. Now will you please tell me what happened in that pulpit.

MARK: I gave my alternate sermon.

TIM: You lost control.

MARK: All right—I lost control, and I'm glad I did.

TIM: A priest should inspire control.

MARK: This morning I felt like a priest for the first time.

TIM: I don't want to hear the "spirit moved you."

MARK: I can't explain it any other way. Why does it have to be explained?

TIM: Because nobody's buying that you're a thoroughbred at the starting gate.

MARK: Then don't try to sell them anything. It was a mystery to me, let it be a mystery to them. Not everything can be explained, for God's sake. The core of the church is extra–scientific and unexplainable.

TIM: Mark—my congregation is not some primitive tribe who'll watch in awe as their priest becomes possessed by some preternatural force. You can't take-off like that and expect to be understood. I've never gotten so many phone calls—never. And the collection went down thirty percent. It's no accident that the collection comes after the sermon. That's like the Neilsen rating.

MARK: Father—if I'm making things difficult for you here,

I'll talk to Monsignor Burke and ask him to let you off the hook, and I'll go back to the seminary. [*Silence*]

TIM: Let's move on to Lesson II—Consolations. Some of the faculty tell me that you're very active in terms of special projects—the retarded, prisoners, the elderly—but they also say that you have a hard time communicating empathy to an average person in pain. Do you feel empathy?

MARK: Yes—I just don't know what to say. Everything I think of saying sounds so stupid.

TIM: But that's the idea. Consolations should sound stupid so that the party in grief will realize how inconsolable their grief is. Inconsolable grief puts a person in a very exalted position. This feeling of being exalted gets most people through most tragedies. So your responsibility as a priest is to bring common grief to the heights of the inconsolable by saying something inane. Let's give it a try. Hit me with a tragedy.

MARK: What kind?

TIM: A tragedy. Someone from the parish pulls you aside after mass and says . . .

MARK: Uh . . . My mother passed away last night, Father.

TIM: Presuming you knew the deceased and she was over seventy, obviously you'd say, "She had a good life." If she was sick, you'd say, "It was merciful."

MARK: Even I could think of something better than that.

TIM: You're not supposed to. Keep it simple and stupid. This is one of the few areas where stupid is smart. Give me another tragedy.
[MARK *thinks*]
Hurry—just pick one out of the pool of human experience and lay it on me.

MARK: My baby died in his crib last night.

TIM: That's awful.

MARK: Is that what you'd say?

TIM: What made you think of something like that?

MARK: You said a tragedy.

TIM: Wow—you really get into it.

MARK: You told me . . .

TIM: Let me see. If the mother was young, you could say, "You can have another."

MARK: Like an hors d'oeuvre.

TIM: Also, you could say he went straight to heaven.

MARK: I'd rather not say anything.

TIM: But you have to say something.

MARK: Why? Why do I have to *say* something? Can't I just listen?

TIM: No. Now let me give you one. My father beats me.

MARK: Now I'm supposed to say something inane?

TIM: Right.

MARK: Okay—your father beats you. Let me think. Uh . . . You don't have any scars, you'd never know it.

TIM: I go to school with black eyes.

MARK: Catholic school?

TIM: What difference would that make?

MARK: Well—they're always fighting in Catholic schools so they all have black eyes—you must fit right in.

TIM: He's left us. We don't know if he's dead or alive.

MARK: Well—that's okay. Who needs a sadist like that for a father. How am I doing?

TIM: My mother's remarried. I hate her new husband.

MARK: Why?

TIM: The church says she can't remarry unless it's certain her first husband is dead.

MARK: That's no reason to hate him.

TIM: I cry myself to sleep because I'm sure she's going to hell.

MARK: Do you believe there can be such a thing as hell?

TIM: After a while—I just wouldn't talk to her.

MARK: You talk to her now—don't you?

TIM: She died and we hadn't exchanged a word in two years.

MARK: You bastard.

TIM: Is that all you have to say?

MARK: Go on. I'm listening.

TIM: I went into the preparatory seminary when I was thirteen. I believed everything I was taught. Followed all the rules—to the letter. I wanted everyone to be perfect. Especially my mother. When I thought she wasn't, I cut her off. She'd write—she'd call—I never answered. Once she called, and I came so close—I had the phone in my hand. But I hung up. Three weeks later, she was dead. You asked me if I believed there's such a thing as hell. There are hints of it on earth.
[MARK *puts his hand on* TIM's *shoulder*]
That's enough on consolations. Let's move on to Lesson III—Converts. [*House phone buzzes.* TIM *presses button*] Yes Margaret . . . Oh no . . . How does he sound? . . . Oh for . . . Okay—thank you, Margaret [*Presses hold button*] Mark—could you excuse me for a minute. This is private.

MARK: Should I leave for the day?

TIM: No—wait in the kitchen. Margaret's doing some work there and she'd love the company. I shouldn't be long.
[MARK *exits.* TIM *presses button*]
Hello, Tom. Glad you called. I was just thinking about you. Listen—we never did get a chance to look at those

pictures from Yugoslavia . . . Could you get ahold of your sister . . . Saturday sounds great . . . All right—see you then, Tom . . . Pardon me? . . . Yes, Mark Dolson did give a sermon. I would have invited you but . . . Yes —I think he did say something about the purpose of the church is to become obsolete, but I'm sure he meant it as a joke . . . No—nobody laughed . . . Tom—I'm sure all of our jobs will be safe for at least another five hundred years . . . It only *sounded* radical . . . Tom—the fact is Mark didn't say anything he didn't have a right to say. Even the faculty said that . . . Yes—I'll send him over to you but you don't need to talk to him about the sermon. I've already shown him what he did wrong . . . It's not? . . . What do you want to see him about? . . . I see . . . But he's always alone . . . I think he defended them because he felt they had a right to change. I really don't think it was anything more than that . . . Yes—I know you like to be sure . . . Yes—I'll send him over to you. See you Saturday, Tom. [*He hangs up, calling offstage*] Mark —come in here.

MARK: [*From offstage*] I'm helping Margaret with the dishes.

TIM: Never mind about the dishes. Come in here now. It's important.

MARK: [*As he enters*] I just have a few more pots . . .

TIM: Monsignor Burke wants to see you as soon as I'm through with you.

MARK: He's upset about the sermon.

TIM: He says it's not about the sermon.

MARK: It's not?

TIM: Monsignor Burke has appointments with several seminarians and now—you.

MARK: Why?

TIM: Some dress funny—others hang out together too much—

MARK: What did I do?

TIM: It seems you were too vehement in your defense of Frank Kearney and Alfred Virasi.

MARK: He's nuts.

TIM: That's just the kind of intelligent approach he's hoping you'll resort to.

MARK: Do I have to put up with this? Can't I see the bishop?

TIM: The bishop is so paranoid about this Frank and Alfred business, he wishes all the altar boys were girls, so he'll let Burke do what he wants.

MARK: What do you think he's going to ask me?

TIM: It's hard to say. These interviews change according to the person he's inter . . . Let's do it.

MARK: What?

TIM: The interview. I'll play Monsignor Burke and you play you.

MARK: I shouldn't have to go through this—at all.

TIM: Mark—relax. You don't have anything to be afraid of—do you? Come on—just go out and come in like you're coming for the interview.

MARK: I don't want to play a psycho game.

TIM: Mark—you have to go through this with as much grace and tact as you can. You can't afford a repeat of your last encounter with him.

MARK: [*Pause*] All right. [MARK *goes off and reenters as if coming in for his interview with Monsignor Burke*]

TIM: [*As* BURKE] Good day, Dolson.

MARK: [*Laughing at the apparent accuracy of the impersonation*] Hello, Monsignor Burke.

TIM: [*As* BURKE] You're late.

MARK: I am? Well—sorry—I've been fasting all week and meditating every night so time and space are . . .

TIM: That's very interesting, Dolson. Have you considered a career in a contemplative order?

MARK: Funny you should say that. Father Farley suggested that very thing to me just today.

TIM: [*As* BURKE] Well—he manages to have a few good ideas every so often. [*As himself*] Leave me out of this. [*As* BURKE] Now—I'd like to ask you a few questions. My first question has to do with Frank Kearney and Alfred Virasi.

MARK: He wouldn't get into that right away.

TIM: [*As himself*] Yes, he would. He's a busy man.

MARK: If he's so busy, he can skip my interview.

TIM: [*As himself*] All right—have it your way. [*As* BURKE] How's your family?

MARK: Fine—thank you.

TIM: [*As* BURKE] There's one thing I've always been curious about, Dolson, in regards to your family life. Why did you leave home at sixteen?

MARK: I wanted to be on my own.

TIM: But so young. Was there something at home pushing you out?

MARK: I don't think I was aware of it at the time, but there was a silence in my house that . . . crushed me. There were choruses going on inside of me, and at dinner we all chewed and clanked—and there were times I thought the fork would melt right in my hand.

TIM: So you left?

MARK: Yes.

TIM: And they let you go?

MARK: I think they were relieved.

TIM: Where did you go?

MARK: [*Pause*] What were you asking about Frank and Alfred?

TIM: [*As* BURKE] Well . . . I have been wondering why you reacted so strongly to the . . . suggestion they take a year off from their studies.

MARK: It was not a suggestion—it was a demand. They did not take a year off—you kicked them out.

TIM: All right—if you want to be direct. [*As* BURKE] Do you think priests should be allowed to sleep together?

MARK: They weren't priests—they weren't even deacons. A vow of celibacy was far off for them.

TIM: [*As* BURKE] Do you think such practices are easily dispensed with?

MARK: Is your question something along the lines of, "How you gonna keep 'em down on the farm after they've seen Paree?"

TIM: [*As* BURKE] Stop your verbal acrobatics and give a response to whatever you interpret my question to be.

MARK: Yes—I think Frank and Alfred would have stayed down on the farm after they had seen "Paree."

TIM: [*As* BURKE] How do you know?

MARK: I said I "think." I did not say I know.

TIM: [*As* BURKE] Let me ask my next question in your native tongue. Have *you* ever seen "Paree"? [*Silence*] And if you have seen "Paree," were they "Parisiettes" or Parisians?

MARK: [*Long pause*] Both.

TIM: [*As himself*] Really?

MARK: That's it—no more. You were shocked.

TIM: I was playing Monsignor Burke. Both?

MARK: Yes—women and men—two sexes. Monsignor—before I came to the seminary, I enrolled myself in a three-year orgy that laid waste to every fibre of my character. Does that sound apologetic enough? How about this? Monsignor Burke—please understand—I explored the world by indulging my sexual ambivalence. I searched with my body and I discovered that I could never reconcile my inner emotional world that way. Others have—but my unique, personal and human condition called for another way. So I invite celibacy. I will be happy to stay down on the farm because it's there I will be calm enough to help others and the only real joy in this world is helping other people. I feel determined and perfectly prepared to become a priest. What would he say to that?

TIM: [*As* BURKE] Both?

MARK: Will you stop?

TIM: I'm sorry—it's just that I've never seen you in this light before.

MARK: What light?

TIM: Red light.

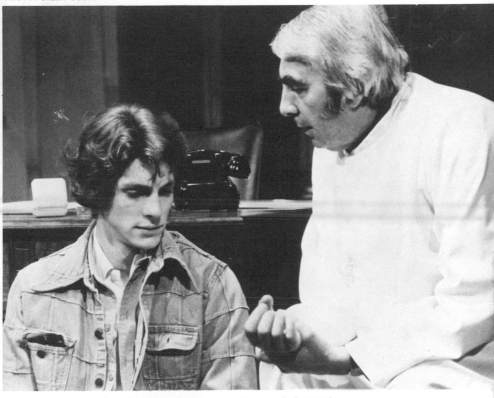

MARK: *(played by Eric Roberts, on left in photo): What are you suggesting I do?*
TIM: *(Milo O'Shea, on right): I'm not suggesting—I'm telling you —don't kick ass.*
MARK: *Better that than to kiss it.*

TIM: *Have* you *ever seen "Paree"?* (Silence) *And if you have seen "Paree," were they "Parisiettes" or Parisians?*
MARK: (Long pause) *Both.*

MARK: *People should be warned about you.*

TIM: *Don't push me.*

MARK: *They all come thinking they're being helped—but really they're just pouring their guts out to a drunk who catalogs their anguish.*

MARK: *Hello, Monsignor . . . Yes, I did give another sermon . . .*
I'm sorry if the people you spoke with thought it was inane. I was
trying to . . . I see . . . Is that decision final? . . . Two weeks . . .
Monsignor—I think what you're doing is a sin. . . .

MARK: And you've *never* been in "red light"?

TIM: By the time my father left and my mother died, I was so confused I didn't want to be near man, woman or piano leg. Celibacy came naturally to me. [*Pause*] Mark— if Monsignor Burke asks you, say, "Yes—I have made love with 'Parisiettes.'"

MARK: That's a half-truth.

TIM: Don't start throwing principles around now, Mark. This is too serious for principles. In the larger scheme of things, he's not that important.

MARK: But the truth is. I won't become a priest on a lie.

TIM: Better that than not at all.

MARK: I can't believe you're saying this. I won't listen.

TIM: All right—don't listen to me. Go in there and do your martyr number. Just leave a forwarding address behind.

MARK: He can't get rid of me.

TIM: He can. Mark—once you're a priest you can fight him all you want. You'll end up hearing confessions in the cornfields of Iowa if you do, but at least give yourself a chance. Make sure you do become a priest. Try it my way. Be diplomatic. Avoid answering questions directly. You can steer the questions. Phrase your answers certain ways . . .

MARK: You mean lie.

TIM: Even Christ said to his apostles, "Be as innocent as doves and as cunning as serpents." Christ said that.

MARK: Does cunning mean lying?

TIM: If you can afford not to be a priest—tell the truth. If you want to be a priest—lie. [*Silence*] Mark—I want you to be a priest. I asked for you.

MARK: You asked for me? You said . . .

TIM: I know. I told you Monsignor Burke made me do this—but he didn't. I asked him to let me help you.

MARK: Why?

TIM: Because you're a lunatic. And the church needs lunatics— And you are one of those priceless lunatics that come along every so often and makes the church alive. The only problem with lunatics is that they don't know how to survive. I do. [*Pause. Holds out his keys*] Here—take my car.
[MARK *takes the keys and exits*]

END OF ACT ONE

ACT TWO

Later. The office. TIM *is waiting. He pours a drink. House phone buzzes.*

TIM: Yes Margaret . . . Yes—Yes—send him in. [MARK *enters. He returns the keys in silence*]
Well? What happened?

MARK: It was great!

TIM: What happened?

MARK: What a feeling!

TIM: What did you say?

MARK: I just sat there with my arm flung over the back of the chair.

TIM: You shouldn't have done that. You might have antagonized him.

MARK: I was just being confident.

TIM: Nothing is more antagonistic than confidence.

MARK: What should I have done? Hugged myself and rocked back and forth.

TIM: Just tell me what happened.

MARK: Everything's fine.

TIM: He didn't ask you.

MARK: He did.

TIM: Oh—I'm sorry. You had to lie. But you see, these things . . .

MARK: I didn't lie.

TIM: You didn't?

MARK: I told him the truth.

TIM: You told him the truth.

MARK: I had to.

TIM: What do you mean you had to?

MARK: It's all right.

TIM: Did he ask about me?

MARK: Yes—he wanted to know if you knew, and I told him you did, but you thought it was just fine because you've given up Margaret for Mr. Hartigan.

44

TIM: Mark—

MARK: Relax—we stayed clear of you.

TIM: I wish you had listened to me.

MARK: Why? Everything's fine. You were wrong about him. And you were wrong about lying.

TIM: I was wrong? All right—fine. Just tell me—after you said "both" what did he say?

MARK: He said, "Thank you for being so honest—good-day."

TIM: That's all he said?

MARK: Yes. Isn't that great?

TIM: "Thank you for being so honest—good-day."

MARK: Right. You see?

TIM: "Thank you for being so honest. Good-day."

MARK: Why are you repeating what he said? [*Silence*] Now don't start reading into it. I mean—why would he thank me for being honest if he didn't . . . No—I'm not going to dissect it . . . You interpret it your way and I'll . . . I'll . . . [MARK *stops—silence*] "Thank you for being so honest—good-day." [*Pause*] I'm in trouble. God—I am so deaf. He sent me to your dialogue sermon and it all seemed very innocent. He expelled Frank and Alfred and called it "taking a leave of absence." And now—"Thank you for being so honest—good-day," which means he's going to get rid of me—isn't he? Isn't he? [*Silence*] Will you help me?

45

TIM: I won't have any influence over Monsignor Burke now.

MARK: Why not?

TIM: You told the truth. If I defend you to him, the same thing that's happening to you would happen to me.

MARK: But it's wrong. Burke gets away with this crap because only one or two people will say anything. The whole parish should get after him. He can't implicate the entire parish.

TIM: True—but . . .

MARK: You said the people in your parish can influence him.

TIM: They can . . .

MARK: And you have influence over them.

TIM: I do, but . . .

MARK: Can't you talk to them about this?

TIM: Well . . . not really . . . I can't.

MARK: Why not?

TIM: Well—because he hasn't done anything yet. He's just asked you a few questions.

MARK: But we both know he will do something. And by the time he does it will be too late to get their help. Will you please talk to them?

TIM: Mark—the fact of the matter is, after that sermon you gave, if I went to the people in my parish and told them Monsignor Burke is about to dump you, they would send him "thank-you" letters.

MARK: Why should it matter what they think of me? There's an issue here.

TIM: You are the issue. [*Pause*] What I would be willing to do is to let you give another sermon.

MARK: What would that do?

TIM: The only way you would stand a chance of getting help from the people in my parish is if you redeemed yourself with them.

MARK: Burke won't let you do that.

TIM: He hasn't told me you can't give any more sermons and if I avoid him for the next week, which is an appealing prospect, I could get away with it.

MARK: Isn't there another way?

TIM: Take the help on my terms, or not at all.

MARK: [*Pause*] I don't know what to say to them.

TIM: We'll call this your redemption sermon. We'll forget Norman Rockwell—we have to go deeper this time. Tell them what made you decide to become a priest. Tell them why you want to help them. I'll pass out reaction sheets so we can see how effective you're being.

MARK: Reaction sheets?

TIM: It'll save wear and tear on the phone. Give them something concrete—like my street corner.

MARK: Your what?

TIM: My . . . never mind. Just think of specifics—a teacher, a best friend—no—we better stay away from best friends for now—a confirmation name, a favorite saint, a pet . . .

MARK: I had a tank of tropical fish. Someone turned up the tank heater and they all boiled.

TIM: That's very interesting—and someday you and I can sit down and relive the whole experience, but right now I don't think boiled fish will melt their hearts. Maybe if you saw *Going My Way* or if a priest saved your little brother's life—something like that—but they can't relate to guppies.

MARK: What *can* they relate to? Bingo? A car sweepstake? The lottery?

TIM: Mark—at ease. [*Pause*] You know—maybe we have this problem in reverse. Maybe it's not so much getting the people to like you as it is getting you to . . . what do you feel for those people you want help from?

MARK: What do you feel for them?

TIM: I'm asking you.

MARK: I can't just *say* what I feel for them.

48

TIM: Yes you can.

MARK: I . . . I love them.

TIM: How do you love them? Intellectually?

MARK: No.

TIM: You really care for them?

MARK: Yes . . . Yes . . . I . . .

TIM: Then why do you offend them?

MARK: I don't mean to.

TIM: Why do you?

MARK: I know what they could be.

TIM: But Mark—what about what they are? What are they to you?

MARK: [*Pause*] They're my family. They get to me. But I don't know how to get to them. Show me.

TIM: [*Pause*] St. Francis got completely undressed in the middle of his town square—he gave all his clothes back to his father, and then he was ready to live. Do the same—be naked—and then talk to them—as if they were one person —talk to them, as if . . . they were me.

MARK: [*To* TIM] I had a tank of tropical fish. Someone turned up the tank heater and they all boiled. [*Moving slowly to the pulpit*] I woke up on a Friday morning—

49

went to feed them—and there they were—all of my beautiful fish floating on the top. Most of them split in two. Others with their eyes hanging out. It looked like violence, but it was such a quiet night. And I remember wishing I had the kind of ears that could hear fish screams because they looked as if they suffered and I wanted so badly to save them. That Sunday in church, I heard that Christ told his apostles to be fishers of men. From then on, I looked at all the people in the church as fish. I was young so I saw them as beautiful tropical fish and so I knew they were all quiet screamers. Church was so quiet. And I thought everyone was boiling. And I wanted the kind of ears that could hear what they were screaming about, because I wanted to save them. [*Pause*] A few years later, the people in the church lost the stained glass look of tropical fish, and they were only catfish to me—overdressed scavengers. So I drowned out whatever I might be able to hear. I made my world—my tank—so hot that I almost split. So now I'm back—listening—listening for the screams of angels. [*The office.* TIM *is drinking and getting drunk as he reads the reactions.* MARK *enters.*]

TIM: Well, Mark—we have loads of reactions.

MARK: Isn't it a little early in the afternoon to be drinking.

TIM: It's just wine. Making wine was Christ's first miracle. He knew what he was doing.

MARK: Did you have breakfast?

TIM: Never mind about that . . .

MARK: You should at least eat something . . .

TIM: You have to hear these reactions.

MARK: I don't want to.

TIM: They're not bad, Mark. I think we might have a chance. Let me just read a few.

MARK: Only if you put the wine down.

TIM: All right—all right—as if you don't have enough causes on your hands. Now! I'll start with the worst and work up to the best. Here's the worst. Are you ready?

MARK: Just read it.

TIM: [*Reading*] "We have no choice but to be catfish with garbage like that being thrown at us." That's the worst and that's not so bad. I know him—Mr. Jennings—he's a jerk—don't worry about him.

MARK: Don't read anymore.

TIM: They get better. "Father—I don't know if we're fish but we're certainly not boiling—it's freezing in that church. Is there any way to turn up the heat, just a little?" It's not negative. "Dear Father Farley—he is a very sweet boy. I had a goldfish once that died from chlorine in the city water so I know just how he feels. I wrote to the city complaining about the amount of chlorine in their water . . ." And she goes on and on, but she likes you. "Father—he shows unusual sensitivity. It's very exciting to watch such a change. You're doing good work." I wrote that. [*He laughs*] No—only kidding. It was from someone in the parish—honest. And the final one—which I hesitate to read to you, but—"Don't take this the wrong way Father, but Mark Dolson is just great. Can he give sermons every Sunday?" What do you think?

MARK: I don't know. What does it mean?

TIM: It means there's hope. They're starting to like you.

MARK: What do we do next?

TIM: Before we do anything, I'm calling up Mr. Jennings and I'm going to tell him what a jerk he is.

MARK: [*Stopping him*] Father—will you just sit down.

TIM: "Garbage"—who does he think he is?

MARK: It's all right.

TIM: He pisses me off.

MARK: Shhhhh.

TIM: Well—he does.

MARK: Don't. He might fight back.

TIM: You think I'm a coward, don't you? Just because I won't make an appeal for you, you think . . .

MARK: Let's not get into it right now.

TIM: Well maybe I will. You don't know what I'll do. [*House phone buzzes*]

MARK: You shouldn't talk to anyone.

TIM: Will you calm down. I'm fine. [*Presses intercom button*] Yes Margaret—oh he is? [*To* MARK] It's "Boyke." Margaret—I just realized I haven't had any breakfast. Could you do something about that? . . . Oh—I have. [TIM *presses hold button*] Mark—I've had breakfast already.

MARK: [*Taking the phone away*] You can't talk to him.

TIM: Yes I can.

MARK: You're going to get in trouble. Give me the phone.

TIM: No. You'll think I'm a coward.

MARK: You're not a coward. Let me talk to him. [*Silence.*
TIM *holds on to the phone*]
Please Father.
[TIM *surrenders the phone*]
Hello, Monsignor—this is Mark Dolson—I'm taking Father Farley's calls right now . . . Yes— we meet more regularly. And I didn't get a chance during our last meeting to thank you for making this special arrangement. It's been . . . Yes, I did give another sermon—I was only hoping to make up for the sermon I had given earlier . . . I'm sorry if the people you spoke with thought it was inane. I was trying to . . . I see . . . Is that decision final? . . . Two weeks . . . Monsignor—I think what you're doing is a sin . . . Yes. I'll tell him to call you.
[*He hangs up*]

TIM: What happened?

MARK: It's official. He wants me out.
[*Pause*] Damn him! It's not right. He can't just make deci-

sions like that. I'm going to fight him. I only have one more Sunday. All I'm asking from you is that you let me make my own appeal in my own way at your mass.

TIM: You can't make an appeal for yourself. That's like nominating yourself for president.

MARK: Who else will do it?

TIM: It's not necessary. You're getting carried away. I'll handle this.

MARK: How?

TIM: I'll call Monsignor Burke.

MARK: No.

TIM: Yes—I'm going to call him right now.

MARK: No—you're drunk.

TIM: I'm at my best when I'm drunk. I'm not your typical drunk. [*As he dials*] I think more clearly—speak more clearly—my vocabullalary is better . . . This is the best possible time for me to speak to Burke. Monsignor Burke please . . . Oh—hello Tom—Mark told me you called . . . Now just slow down, Tom—I can do whatever I want in my parish. Don't presume more authority than you . . . It was a good sermon. Mark has made incredible strides . . . Yes, he told me and I totally disagree with your decision. This whole sexual question is ridiculous. He will keep his vows . . . What? . . . Yes—I'm keeping mine. What are you . . . Tom—there are limits . . . No—I will not be threatened. If I decide Mark gives another sermon, then he'll give a sermon. If I decide to give a sermon about

54

Mark, then that's what I'll do. You are not going to intimidate me with your gestapo tactics. And another thing—I had a terrible time in Yugoslavia. Good-bye Monsignor. [*He hangs up the phone*] I'll do it.

MARK: What?

TIM: I will make an appeal for you.

MARK: You don't mean it. It's the wine . . .

TIM: I do mean it. It's not the wine. I'm going to cash in my popularity stock for power. Monsignor Burke will be flooded with letters and phone calls.

MARK: What do you mean "cash in"? What will happen to you if you make an appeal for me?

TIM: If I make an appeal for you this Sunday, Burke will do everything he can to make sure I'll be in Iowa by Tuesday. But my people won't let anything happen to me. They won't let me go.

MARK: Are you sure?

TIM: Absolutely. I'm not afraid of Burke. I've prayed for that. I've prayed not to be afraid and right here and now I'm not. I'm not afraid . . .

[BLACKOUT. *The church.* TIM *is in the pulpit.*]

TIM: There are all forms of persecution. I'm sure if we watch the 6:00 o'clock news for a week we'd be sure to see almost every kind. But what about the ones that occur right here in this town—or in this parish. The ones we can do something about. Let's think for a moment about the times we thought someone was being persecuted for their race or their religion or their past—and let's just think of how we responded. [*Pause*] Now I know in some cases there's only so much we can do—but did we do that? Let's just think. [*Silence—he watches them*] Now I don't want you to be too hard on yourselves—I'm not trying to impose a sense of guilt on all of you—there are all kinds of reasons a person can't respond completely to an injustice, but still—we should be aware of—or we should find time to . . . well—let's take for example—Mark Dolson. He's being persecuted—perhaps that's too strong a word. He's experiencing some difficulty at the seminary with . . . the higher-ups because . . . because . . . well, because he's young. Which is natural—age has a natural resentment for youth—it just seems to happen. But Mark can take care of himself. You've all seen that for yourselves. I know I have. [*He laughs*] So that really isn't a good example of persecution. The best example of persecution I can think of right now, at this time is—many of you may not know this but I was an abused child. My father would beat me regularly—he would literally send me flying across rooms. Now that's real persecution. So that's something to watch out for—if you know of a child who is being abused, don't be afraid to act. Call the County Task Force at 473-1059. Let us pray.

[*The office.* TIM *is waiting.*]

[MARK *enters.*]

MARK: You wanted to see me.

TIM: Yes. Where did you go?

MARK: To the seminary. To pack.

TIM: What will you do?

MARK: I'm not sure.

TIM: Maybe there's another diocese you might be able to go to. I'll make some inquiries.

MARK: Don't.

TIM: It's worth a try.

MARK: You know it isn't.

TIM: I'm sorry if I got your hopes up. But it won't work. I saw that in their faces. I can tell when they're with me, and they weren't . . . I can ask them for a few dollars—some cake for a bake sale maybe—but that is it. [*Silence*] They aren't what you expect them to be. [*Silence*] I can only give them what they can handle. [*Silence*] They turn quickly. [*Pause*] Whatever I said I'd do was above and beyond the call of duty.

MARK: I understand.

TIM: I don't know if you do. I have a lot at stake. [*Silence*] Not just the Mercedes or this office, but . . . You don't understand.

MARK: All right. I don't understand.

TIM: This is my home. The people know me. They know my favorite colors—the kind of sweaters I like—my favorite wine—[*Smiling*] Do you know what a town in Iowa is like? There might be a Main Street. If there is a movie theatre, it only shows family movies. The people would not understand my humor. They wouldn't talk to me. [*Silence*] I have to talk to people.

MARK: Then why don't you?

TIM: I do. [*Silence*] Well—if you want me to help you find a job or if you ever need a recommendation let me know. [*Smiling*] I have to kick you out now—I have an appointment coming any minute.

MARK: No you don't.

TIM: What?

MARK: You don't have an appointment.

TIM: Are you saying I'm lying?

MARK: Yes.

TIM: Why would I lie about that?

MARK: I don't know why you lie—I can just tell when you do.

TIM: You better go.

MARK: But it's all right. They're all harmless lies. You only do it to spare other people's feelings. Right?

TIM: I liked it better when you weren't saying anything. You have to go. [MARK *doesn't move. Silence*] Whether you believe me or not, I have an appointment coming in here any minute.

58

MARK: An appointment. Really? Which "human condition" is it today? A divorce? An abortion? Or an identity crisis?

TIM: None of your business.

MARK: Why don't you give a break to whoever it is and cancel.

TIM: I know you think you have a right to be angry with me . . .

MARK: I'm not angry with you.

TIM: You are . . . You think I betrayed you.

MARK: What you did or didn't do for me doesn't make any difference. I believed you, because I needed to believe you. I set myself up—that's not your fault. But the people who come to you for help deserve more.

TIM: Don't worry about the people who come to me. They're taken care of.

MARK: You handle them—I've seen it—the way you handled me. You say what everyone needs to hear. Doesn't matter if it's true or if you can back up what you say, as long as you pacify whoever is on the other side of the desk. You'll say anything to get a person in need off your back.

TIM: Get out Mark.

MARK: No. I think I should wait here until your "appointment" comes.

TIM: Would you please leave?

MARK: I should warn whoever it is. People should be warned about you.

TIM: Don't push me.

MARK: They all come thinking they're being helped—but really they're just pouring their guts out to a drunk who catalogs their anguish.

TIM: Get out! [TIM *punches* MARK *in the stomach*] Ow! I think I broke my wrist.

MARK: I'm sorry.

TIM: It's broken—I know it.

MARK: It can't be.

TIM: It bent back.

MARK: You don't know how to punch.

TIM: I never had a reason to.

MARK: Maybe it's sprained. Twirl your arm around.

TIM: What?

MARK: Twirl your arm around. Like this. [*He demonstrates a wide circular motion with his arm.* TIM *copies*]

TIM: What's this supposed to do?

MARK: It's for . . . it . . . it's supposed to . . . I don't know. [*Laughing*] I don't know what it's supposed to do.

TIM: You don't know?

MARK: No . . . [MARK *falls to the floor laughing.* TIM *joins the laughter.* TIM's *laughter turns to tears. Then there is silence*]

TIM: I tried Mark—I wanted to help you—but I need them.

MARK: I understand—I do, but . . . During those three years —whenever someone I loved, loved me, I did everything to keep it constant. Bit by bit—through trial and error—I learned all the rules—what to say—what to give—what to withhold—so I could keep the love constant. But to go through all that—to worry about who's got the upper hand—who's going to change first—it made the love worthless. I found out that the constant is up to me. Promises are broken; friends will be fickle; love goes its own course; and ultimately none of it has to matter. And what you believe has to be more important than what your congregation thinks of you.

TIM: I'm not sure what I believe anymore. [*He looks down and sees his watch.*] Oh my God—I have a mass at 5:20. [*He begins to put on his vestments.*] It's the most attended mass of the day. [*He stops*] I miss the street corner. The heat—the hat. They were just people on their way to somewhere, but they stopped—to listen—to me. And I was enough of a child that I wanted to spread my heart out in front of their faces, but now . . . I don't know what to say to them. I can't face them. I can't.

MARK: Yes. You can. [MARK *dresses* TIM]

TIM: What about you?

MARK: I'll be fine. [MARK *puts stole on* TIM]

TIM: Mark, did you know that when Christ sent his apostles out into the world, he sent them in twos. I think I know why he did that now. [*Pause*] Where will you go?

MARK: Right now, I think I should go back to the seminary, and finish packing. [*Silence—they shake hands—*MARK *exits.*]
[*Lights up on pulpit*]
[TIM *moves from the office to the pulpit*]
[*The church*]

TIM: I haven't prepared anything . . . I just have two announcements and then we'll . . . the first announcement— The Holy Rosary Society is sponsoring a Father and Son breakfast this Thursday . . . I can't . . . I can't do this anymore. [*He crumples the announcements*] Mark Dolson has been expelled from St. Francis Seminary and barred from the priesthood. Right now, without having been ordained, Mark Dolson is a better priest than I am. I've been nothing more than your little windup priest doll. I'm the kind of priest Monsignor Burke wants for you. You must demand better. Prior to his decision to become a priest, Mark made love with women and with men. Monsignor Burke is using this personal and irrelevant data as a way to get rid of Mark. Monsignor Burke is motivated by a need to preserve his position of power. Mark threatens that position. I no longer have any influence over Monsignor Burke. But you do. You do have power. Use it. It's not only his church—this is our church. Fight for it. You and I and Mark must be allowed to help shape the thing that has shaped us. Up to now, my need for your love and approval has kept me silent and inactive. This is the first time I've ever said what I wanted to you. Only now is love possible. Let us . . . Oh—and the second announcement—if I am still here next week, I won't be accepting any more sparkling Burgundy. Let us . . . begin. In the Name of the Father and of the Son and of the Holy Spirit—Amen.

[*Lights fade*]

END OF ACT TWO

BILL C. DAVIS, born in 1952, is a graduate of sixteen years of Catholic schooling. During the 60s and 70s he attended Lourdes High School and Marist College in Poughkeepsie, New York. MASS APPEAL, his first full-length play to be produced in New York, was directed by Geraldine Fitzgerald and opened to wildly enthusiastic critical acclaim. Davis is resident playwright at the Manhattan Theater Club, which staged MASS APPEAL.